Nature's Children

WEASELS

Bill Ivy

GROLIER
EDUCATIONAL

FACTS IN BRIEF

Classification of North American weasels
Class: *Mammalia* (mammals)
Order: *Carnivora* (meat-eaters)
Family: *Mustelidae* (weasel family)
Genus: *Mustela* (weasels)
Species: *Mustela frenata* (Long-tailed Weasel); *Mustela nivalis* (Least Weasel); *Mustela erminea* (ermine)

World distribution.   The Long-tailed Weasel is found only in the Americas; the other two species are found in Europe, Asia, Africa and North and South America.

Habitat.   All three occupy a wide variety of terrains.

Distinctive physical characteristics.   Long slender body; short legs; strong odor; size and coloration vary with species.

Habits.   Solitary; most active at night; store food.

Diet.   Birds, insects and small mammals.

Published originally as
"Getting to Know . . . Nature's Children."

This series is approved and recommended
by the Federation of Ontario Naturalists.

This library reinforced edition is available exclusively from:

GROLIER
EDUCATIONAL

Sherman Turnpike, Danbury, Connecticut 06816

Contents

Few animals have such a poor reputation as weasels. It seems that no one loves them. To call someone a "weasel" is quite an insult, since weasels are thought to be cruel and sneaky. But do weasels really deserve all this bad publicity?

If you took a close look at a weasel you might be in for a surprise. The first thing you would notice would be the weasel's bright black eyes and intelligent-looking face. It doesn't look sneaky at all—just alert and watchful. A closer look at how this small creature lives might reveal even more surprises.

Unlikely Relatives

The weasel is a member of a very large and interesting animal family. It bears a strong family resemblance to its closest cousins—the fisher, marten and mink— but some of its more distant relatives might come as a surprise. Among these are the skunk, badger, otter and wolverine.

One thing that most members of this family have in common is beautiful, silky coats.

The markings on the face of southern Long-tailed Weasels have earned them the name "bridled weasel."

Long-tailed Weasel dressed in its winter finery.

6

Three Weasels

Weasels live in most of North America, Europe and Asia. Some even live as far south as South America and northern Africa.

Although there are about ten different kinds of weasels in the world, only three make their home in Canada and the United States—the Long-tailed Weasel, the ermine and the Least Weasel.

Least Weasel

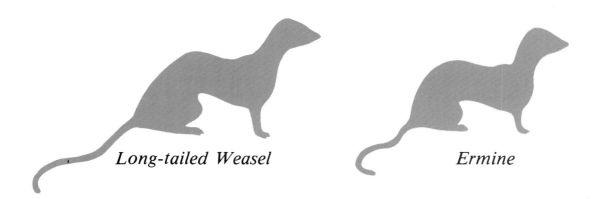

Long-tailed Weasel   *Ermine*

Even though it is North America's largest weasel, the Long-tailed Weasel weighs less than half a kilogram (one pound)!

Long-tailed Weasel

Can you guess how the Long-tailed Weasel got its name? Of course—because it has a very long tail, almost a third of its total length. From the tip of its nose to the end of this long tail, a male Long-tailed Weasel measures about 55 centimetres (21 inches). This makes it the largest of the three North American weasels. The female is considerably smaller than the male.

In the summer, the Long-tailed Weasel's fur is cinnamon-brown on the upper part with yellowish white undersides. In the southern part of its range it bears a black-and-white face mask that looks rather like a bridle and has earned it the name of "bridled weasel."

The Long-tailed Weasel is active at night and does its sleeping during the day. It is a good swimmer and always lives close to water.

Where Long-tailed Weasels live in North America.

The Long-tailed Weasel can climb a tree quietly enough to surprise a roosting bird.

The Ermine

Some people think that the ermine is white all year round. This is not so. In the summer, the ermine is a lovely chocolate brown color with white front feet and belly. Its black-tipped tail is not very long and accounts for only one-quarter of its total length of 21 to 33 centimetres (8-13 inches).

Unlike the other two weasels that live in North America, the ermine is sometimes active during the day. But like the others, it is very fearless and will not hesitate to climb a tree or take to the water while hunting. This bold little creature will sometimes even venture into a cabin to dine on leftover kitchen scraps.

Where ermine live in North America.

The ermine is also known as the Short-tailed Weasel.

Least Weasel

The Least Weasel is tiny, as its name suggests. Only 18 to 20 centimetres (7-8 inches) long and weighing about 43 grams (one and a half ounces), it is one of the smallest meat-eaters in the world. It is no larger than many of the mice it hunts and smaller than some of its prey. Like most weasels, though, it is bold and fearless. In fact its Latin name *rixosa* means quarrelsome.

The Least Weasel is quite rare and is very seldom seen. It has an attractive walnut-brown color set off by bright white underparts and feet.

Where Least Weasels live in North America.

Because of its small size, the Least Weasel is also called the pygmy weasel.

Weasel Homes

Weasels live in grasslands, woods, marshes and farmlands—wherever there is plenty of food.

Some live in hollow logs and stumps, while others take over other animals' underground burrows and "redecorate" them. Usually this means enlarging the den and adding extra entrances. When they are done the den may have three rooms—a bedroom, toilet and food storage room. To make its bedroom comfortable, the weasel may line it with grass and with fur plucked from its prey (which often includes the burrow's previous owner!).

If no natural site is available, weasels will sometimes move in with people. They will make their homes in the crawl spaces under buildings or in unused corners of barns.

Who goes there? (Least Weasel)

Where's the Weasel?

If you have ever seen a weasel in the wild consider yourself lucky—few people have. Why are weasels so difficult to spot? One reason is that they are usually active after sunset. Another is their small size and speediness. Even the largest of the weasels usually weighs less than 270 grams (half a pound), and this small bundle rarely walks—it bounds. So if you are walking in the country one evening and see a small furry blur out of the corner of your eye, try to take a closer look. It might be a weasel.

The weasel knows how to stay out of sight. Although you do not see it, chances are it is watching you.

Change of Clothes

Just like you, weasels have different winter and summer wardrobes. During the summer they have a rich brown coat with a lighter colored belly. But in the fall, the fur on their heads, backs and sides takes on a "salt and pepper" look. Gradually, as winter approaches, the brown hairs are shed, and white hairs grow in their place.

Weasels' winter coats blend in perfectly with the snow. This allows them to scamper about without being seen. Not only can they sneak up on their prey with ease but also they are less visible to their enemies.

When spring comes, dark hairs once again appear along the weasels' backs and sides. Before too long, they are fully outfitted in their summer browns.

In the southern parts of their range where snow rarely falls, weasels do not need a white winter coat. They wear their brown coats all year round.

Two Layered Coat

No matter what the time of year, weasels always have a double fur coat. Close to the weasel's body is a layer of thick inner fur. This keeps in body heat in the winter. To keep water off this layer of fur, the weasel has long guard hairs that are over the underfur.

As you might expect, the weasel's summer coat is much shorter and less dense than its winter coat. After all, who needs a big fur coat in mid-summer?

Glow-in-the-dark eyes.

Little Stinker

Would you believe that any animal could smell worse than a skunk? Some people claim that weasels do! Their foul-smelling odor is caused by a liquid known as musk. Unlike skunks, weasels cannot spray their enemies with musk. However, the terrible smell they give off when frightened or excited is enough to discourage many animals from attacking.

Weasels also use their musk to mark the borders of their hunting area, or territory. Should another weasel of the same sex wander inside these boundaries, the musk warns the intruder that it is trespassing and is not welcome. The scent is a secret message for other weasels. It tells them who lives there, how long ago they last visited this particular spot, and whether they are male or female. Female weasels also use musk to attract a mate.

When not raising a family, a weasel prefers to live alone.

Big Appetite

Imagine eating half your weight in food a day. That would mean that you would need 18 kilograms (40 pounds) of food a day if you weighed 36 kilograms (80 pounds). And that would be like eating 160 big hamburgers a day. Whew!

Although weasels are much smaller than we are, they *do* eat half their weight in food a day. As you can imagine, finding all that food is hard work.

Weasels do not eat vegetables. Only meat will do. The Least Weasel only eats mice, voles, insects and some amphibians. The ermine and Long-tailed Weasel also eat small rodents and insects, but squirrels, birds, eggs, reptiles, worms and rabbits add variety to their menu.

While hunting, the weasel relies even more on its keen sense of smell than on its eyesight.

Frozen Food

Just as squirrels gather nuts in the fall, weasels build up a large food supply for the winter. To do this, they take more prey than they can eat at one time. This helps to explain the weasel's reputation for being greedy.

The uneaten food is stored away in their burrow's special food storage room. To discourage any freeloaders from stealing, weasels scent this meat with their foul-smelling musk. This makes it very unappetizing to others.

Keeping stored food fresh is no problem. Because it is cold, the meat freezes. When weasels want to eat, they bring the frozen meat into their fur and grass-lined bedrooms. Soon, their body heat thaws the meat and they can eat. But however much food weasels store, they almost always run out. To find more, they hunt all winter long.

Tiny Terror

When it comes to hunting, you have to admire weasels. Few animals can match their skill and daring. They show little fear, and many will not hesitate to attack animals much bigger than they are.

Considering their small size, weasels are incredibly strong and agile. A weasel has no difficulty dragging a rabbit. To match this feat a lion would have to haul an elephant!

When chasing smaller game, weasels have a great advantage over larger predators. Their slender, tube-like bodies not only allow them to move with lightning speed, but they can also follow their prey right into its den, using their whiskers to help navigate through the narrow tunnels.

Tireless hunters, weasels spend most of their waking hours on the prowl, sometimes moving so silently that they can actually snatch a bird resting on its perch! No wonder they are considered to be among the best hunters in the world.

Weasel paw prints

Front

Back

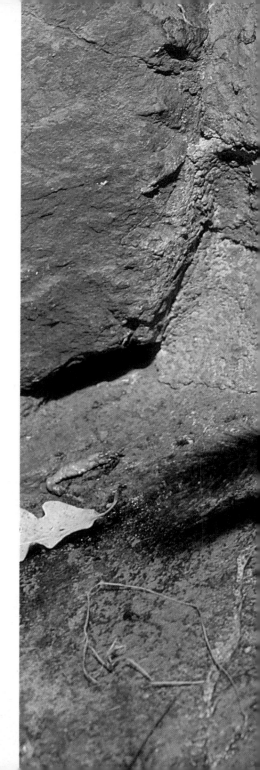

Mating Season

To attract a mate, the female deposits her musk around her home territory. This musk may smell awful to us, but to a male weasel it is a very attractive scent.

The Long-tailed Weasel and ermine mate in the summer, but the female does not give birth until the following spring. Least Weasels often mate in January or February and give birth the same spring. Sometimes they will have another litter later in the summer.

Where snow cover is uncommon, the ermine may remain brown all year.

Meet the Babies

Before her babies are born, the female weasel prepares a nursery. Usually she digs out a special chamber in her den and makes a nest out of grass, feathers and fur. In this soft, warm nest three to 12 young are born.

What peculiar looking babies they are! Each one is pink and wrinkled. Their eyes and ears are sealed shut. They are entirely helpless and dependent on their mother.

At first the weasel babies live solely on their mother's milk. But before too long they are ready for solid food. The young weasels have an enormous appetite. They eat more than their body weight each day. Supplying all this food keeps their mother very busy.

Bright-eyed babies.

Play School

Once their eyes open at four to five weeks, the young weasels are very playful. They jump and tumble with each other, squeaking and squealing as they attack. Playing together is more than just fun. It helps to build the young weasels' muscles and teaches them valuable lessons about hunting. After all, pouncing on a brother or sister is not all that different from attacking a mouse.

But although the young weasels get stronger and more agile by the day, their mother is very protective of them. If any predator comes near, the mother weasel will courageously try to chase it off. She may even carry the babies away from danger one by one in her mouth.

The young grow very quickly. By age two to three months, they leave their mother and begin to hunt for themselves.

Catch Them If You Can

Tooth for tooth and gram for gram, the weasel is among the most ferocious animals in the world. What it lacks in size it more than makes up for in courage and boldness. Unbelievable as it may seem, a weasel no bigger than a kitten will attack a bear or a man standing in the way of its young.

Few animals care to tangle with such a determined foe. However, the weasel's own relatives—the mink, marten and fisher—are equally fierce and quick. These relatives will hunt weasels, as will foxes, bobcats, lynx, coyotes, wolves and larger hawks and owls.

Fortunately, the weasel has a great advantage over most of its enemies. It has an amazing ability to escape through the tiniest of openings. Have you ever heard the term "to weasel out of it"? This expression means to get out of something you do not want to do. It is easy to see how this saying began since nobody can "weasel" out of trouble like a weasel! Thanks to this amazing ability, weasels may live to be five to six years old in the wild.

Opposite page:

Weasels often sit on their haunches to get a better view of the world around them.

Friend Not Foe

Biologists tell us that if it were not for weasels, rats and mice would multiply so rapidly that they would overrun the world. As it is, mice cost us a tremendous amount each year in damaged crops. Weasels know what to do with these pests. One male alone can kill at least 500 mice a year! Their ability to catch small rodents would put any cat to shame. They are such good mousers, in fact, that their family name *Mustelidae* means "those who carry off mice."

Weasel Lore

North America's Native People have always had great respect for the weasel's fiery spirit. The Indians believed that the capturing of a weasel promised good fortune. In Inuit culture, some consider it good luck to have a weasel cross their path, and a young hunter sometimes carries a weasel pelt on his belt in the hope that he will inherit some of this animal's hunting skills.

Should a weasel ever race by you, try this trick. Stay perfectly still and make a squeaking sound by kissing the back of your hand. Chances are its curiosity will win out and it will reappear. You might just get a better look at one of nature's most graceful but secretive mammals.

Words to Know

Amphibians   A group of animals that includes such animals as frogs.

Biologist   Scientist who studies animals and plants.

Burrow   A hole in the ground dug by an animal to be used as a home.

Den   Animal home.

Litter   Young animals born together.

Marsh   Soft wet land.

Mate   To come together to produce young.

Mating season   Time of year during which animals mate.

Musk   A strong-smelling odor produced by some animals.

Predator   Animal that lives by hunting others for food.

Reptiles   A group of animals that includes such animals as snakes, lizards and turtles.

Territory   Area that an animal or group of animals lives in and often defends from other animals of the same kind.

INDEX

Cover Photo: Wayne Lankinen (Valan Photos)

Photo Credits: Phil Dotson (National Audubon Society Collection/Miller Services), pages 4, 7, 12-13; Gregory Dimijian (National Audubon Society Collection/Miller Services), page 8; Barry Griffiths (Network Stock Photo File), page 11; Tom McHugh (National Audubon Society Collection/Miller Services), pages 14, 25, 35; Alvin E. Staffan (National Audubon Society Collection/Miller Services), page 17; Norman Lightfoot (Eco-Art Productions), page 18; Thomas Kitchin (Valan Photos), page 21; Wayne Lankinen (Valan Photos), pages 22, 45; Mildred McPhee (Valan Photos), page 27; Leonard Lee Rue III (National Audubon Society Collection/Miller Services), page 28; C.G. Hampson (Valan Photos), pages 32-33; Alan Carey (National Audubon Society Collection/Miller Services), pages 36, 41; G.R. Higbee (National Audubon Society Collection/Miller Services), page 42.

Printed and Bound in Italy by Lego Sp.